Vahni Capildeo's multilingual, cross-genre writing is grounded in time experienced through place. Her DPhil in Old Norse literature and translation theory, her travels, and her Indian diaspora/Caribbean background deepen the voices in the landscapes that inspire her. Her poetry (six books and four pamphlets) includes *Measures of Expatriation*, awarded the Forward Prize for Best Collection in 2016. She has worked in academia; in culture for development, with Commonwealth Writers; and as an Oxford English Dictionary lexicographer. Capildeo held the Judith E. Wilson Poetry Fellowship and the Harper-Wood Studentship at Cambridge. She is currently a Douglas Caster Cultural Fellow at the University of Leeds.

Also by Vahni Capildeo
from Carcanet Press

Measures of Expatriation

VAHNI CAPILDEO

VENUS as a BEAR

CARCANET

First published in Great Britain in 2018
by
Carcanet Press Limited
Alliance House, 30 Cross Street
Manchester M2 7AQ

Text copyright © Vahni Capildeo, 2018.

The right of Vahni Capildeo to be identified as the author
of this work has been asserted by her in accordance with the
Copyright, Designs and Patents Act of 1988.

Book design: Luke Allan. Printed by SRP Ltd.
A CIP catalogue record for this book is available from
the British Library, ISBN 9781784105549.

The publisher acknowledges financial assistance
from Arts Council England.

CONTENTS

CREATURES

Welcome   13
Day, with Hawk   14
Stone Curlew (Looking for a)   15
Gilberte Said Lizards   17
Brant Geese   20
The Pets of Others   21
Catifesto   22
They (May Forget (Their Names (If Let Out)))   23

SHAMELESS ACTS OF EKPHRASIS

Saying Yes to Zeus   25
The Last Night, A Nightingale   26
Museum Stands In   27
A Table of My Own   28
Latona and Her Children   29
Dog or Wolf   30
Through & Through   31
Circle   35
Kiskadee   36
Venus as a Bear: The Cabin Boy's Prayer   37
The Antonine Wall   38

LANGUES/TONGUES

Leaves/Feuilles/Falls   42
Two Foreign   46
Four Presents with Petrarch   47
After Catullus 5   50
Bullshit   52

After *Hávamál* 53

Evolving @ 54

Novena Body Parts 55

SEA HERE

Tic Tac Toe 60

Tending 61

Salthill Blue for Mr Laughlin 62

Inishbofin: I 63

Inishbofin: II 64

Inishbofin: III 65

Inishbofin: IV 66

Seastairway 67

Waterloo, Trinidad 69

SOME THINGS

Strong as Roses 71

Trinidad Sugar 72

Moss, for Maya 73

Orchids, for Maya 74

Seed, for Maya 76

Heirloom Rose, for Maya 77

Fossil Trade, for Maya 79

Björk / Birch Tree 80

Crossing Borders 82

LIKE...LIKE...

Charlotte Street 88

& When Desire for Air... 89

She Sells...by the Sea Shore 90

Innocents 91

Riddles 93

MUSIC/AVANT TOUTE CHOSE

The Magnificent Pigs of Thetford   97

Catgut   101

When Sitting in the Kitchen Is Like Being…   102

The Seething Sea   103

Envoi   104

Acknowledgements   107

Index of Places   109

L'on ne peut sortir d'arbre par des moyens d'arbre.

Francis Ponge
'Faune et Flore', *Le parti pris des choses* (1942)

A not torn rose-wood color. If it is not dangerous then a pleasure and more than any other if it is cheap is not cheaper. The amusing side is that the sooner there are no fewer the more certain is the necessity dwindled. Supposing that the case contained rose-wood and a color. Supposing that there was no reason for a distress and more likely for a number, supposing that there was no astonishment, is it not necessary to mingle astonishment.

Gertrude Stein
'A Piece of Coffee' in 'Objects', *Tender Buttons* (1914)

for Fern Broome Richards

Venus as a Bear

WELCOME

Early lambs   born some hours ago
curls canalled   crimson-ridged
too new to agitate   won't stick heads through
the well-adapted fence   or wait on treats
but stay   succeed in standing
funny fuzzy   valuable wedges
cave painting   hand-smoothed treasures
A fine sound   the ewes bellowing
a hybrid flock   individual faces
strength in the legs   warmth in the shed

DAY, WITH HAWK

for K.M. Grant

Here among witch-hazels I miss
the peregrine we met just once.
Like the fire from bare twigs that twists
a floral kiss on winter's neck,
He stunned me so I'm hanging on
to language by its clichés, pushed
to singer-songwrite fingernails
down a tumbling slate precipice.
I would call Him chestnut-stippled,
light on the arm, I want to say,
the non-urgent flexing of chest
muscles making a snow-champion's
balance; and bad old hierarchy
doffs its executioner's garb
to rise with the word, princely. Love,
this is; no poem. What is the term
for the gathering of one falcon?
An embarrassment of poets.
An adoration. An abyss.

STONE CURLEW (LOOKING FOR A)

Whistled you up, buttercup-eyes,
Dikkops, yellow-legs,
in fantasy
clumping the Brecks
Thick-Legs, your nietzschean dancing;
wished for
that visitation of pre-human time
your kind
shames, transforms our night
into net and nocturnes
moves devoid of
soundtracks
arrowed ahead of
deliberate shrieks
flouting sight's site as
the governing sense.

Wait a summerlong day for you.
Clumsy
in our claim to a hide.
Waited,
and so much interposed itself.
Moth, and grass. Both feathers, both tigers.
A fade of rabbits; subtle, amiable.
So much interposition.
Always, somewhere, you.
Pale, stripe, brush, pile, head, down.
This was also you.
Moth in and out of a jar.
Some things don't want to be known.
Inside a hut. Inside a pile of brush.

Suddenly, the flock –
and our hearts died in us, and lifted.
For we had seen you
behaving wrongly for the season.
You were leaving for Spain,
when you were required in the books
and by your own need for generation
to bide a while;
to lay, and guard, and plain.

GILBERTE SAID LIZARDS

for Gilberte O'Sullivan

I. BORDER

In the beginning
were the lizards
or some thing
going digging
dark holes
to bodily circumference,
slanting those
routes under
sand below windows.
Cacti flower
in their no-longer-bed,
scarlet, starrier
than ixora or radio
aerial signals.
Lizards, she said.

II. TERRAZZO

Infancy was lizard.
Lizard was mutability.
Mortality was lizard.
Delicate eschatology,
detachable tail,
surface reversibility.
Find the frail
little-finger-length corpse
as you learn to crawl.
Reach into a box:
a raw stump leaps up,
torso sorts itself out.

Skate fast, faster – stop,
grab a post:
fastener-heart jumps
cased in your fist;
you gasping; eyes bulging;
what face your clutch expressed.

III. DRIVEWAY

Why this ixora
tall as any other
grew by nature sicklier:
leathery, sombre
foliage sparser
along its rigging; scarcer
still, unusual, paler,
more pointed, off-pink
westering flowers
more prized than picked,
persistent as housewives
thinking in lipstick
consistent with lives
whose positional hazards
are hidden deliveries,
why from such branches this lizard
fell – I don't know,
and brood on, entwisted.

IV. EVERYWHERE AS NOWHERE

Gilberte brings
cocoa-pod eyes,
ink milk,
lime juice,
songs that brink
on flippant choice:
blink, sink,
cling, go,
gecko, skink.
Orange through blue,
punk to decadence,
skins show,
falling, some sense
of death as life's outward;
and so lizard blends.

BRANT GEESE

open a bubble of babble
swagger and swallow a vowel
turd it turn it shine it slime it
give it wings stretch it – a gaggle,
putting it bluntly: goose to geese,
a Brant goose, a burnt bird, a bit
shorter than other editions
of goose; compact, charcoal; side-on
pushing a shape like a cornea,
honking onyx, flying saucer
confusable with barnacles,
those goose-cousins considered fish
by Friday-famished Christians
whose geese grew on trees, under seas,
spawning anyhow except eggs –
those are not these; though goose occurs
seldom as one, but by volumes,
named in a northern tongue as marked
by fire; brought down by shooters
eyed to cut holes in ice.

THE PETS OF OTHERS

Turtle thrashes opposite the dishwasher,
climbs the water breakline, while the rocks
wait artificially; what sand is needed
being supposable only from flippers
in action, while the chin lifts; she meets the eyes
of tall and dry onlookers. Her red streaks seem
so powerful, a punishable woman's!
Yet compassion flows pointlessly towards her,
like a sable marram dune shifting to make valleys
in which some find rest, from which the sea cannot be glimpsed,
or a way out predicted. Her eggs will come
unfertilised, after how much compulsive
thrashing; and she will be saved from eating them
by her warm-handed keepers, who'd love her wild.

CATIFESTO

for Metu Miller

Familiar in a household of one.
A safte Cleopatrician.
Aesthetic chest-sitter.
Licker, shredder and examiner
of whatsoever covers my floors.
At odds and evens with heat
gliding whiskery information
through red walls.
I am my own cat
bite
my work equipment's corners
rub
my moulting hair on sofas
lie
along the top of doors
just when bipeds try to exit
put
nose over tail, am a world
of my own, in my own world
strike
(herewith they do condemn me)
flitting, twitting, trotting things.
Freedom I taste in them, joy.
I loosen my ribs,
roll sound like no others.
A household of one is no stranger.
I have adapted enough.

THEY (MAY FORGET (THEIR NAMES (IF LET OUT)))

petcitement incitement of a pet to excitement
petcitement incitement into the excitement
of being a pet petcitement incitement to be
a pet a fed pet a fleece pet incitement to be
a floorpet a fleapit a carpet a polkadot
blanket pet blanket pet answer brass doorbell what name
tin waterbowl what name thrilled vomitfall polkadot
padded on patted on turded on welcome mat name
turns to no one's reminder walks wilder walks further
downriver from calling calling owner predator
who that who tagalong meaner whose canines further
from food fleece floor flea cloth car poll card dot blank bit door
no no owner owns in nomine domini pet
outruns petfetch petcome will wild default reset

SAYING YES TO ZEUS

Cast of a fifth-century BCE bronze statue.
Ashmolean Museum, Oxford

Tall Zeus, forgive the mean aspect of this standard and static depiction your admirers should find problematic: squared-off toenails, small ears, some parts one shan't mention – for you hold the lightning bolt – but you don't; even that is gone from this bronze copy.

All-seeing Zeus, overlook how we come close: your frown, your sinews, your ankles resemble the elderly athlete the museum claims this figure might be. You love mortality.

Dear Zeus. Our clouded heads forgot: the copy, and the copier, sportsman, model, statue, maker, are your originals. Through you we move. Through us, you move.

Lord of lightning, spinal fire that sexes the brain, nuclear waste: a great many feathers puncture my breast from within; as I rip, ridding myself of them, finding I cannot free myself, they vault outwards. Like everything, I am in your grasp and also flying.

It strikes me you are sometimes kind.

THE LAST NIGHT, A NIGHTINGALE

Red-vented Bulbul. Gouache on paper, early nineteenth
century. Ashmolean Museum, Oxford

You begin with a design:
the artist's strokes
a kind of preening that elicits
frictive glosses from your close-up wings.
Whoever drew you also caged you,
this freehand desert-colour time-box
partly pinkish, like your eggshells.
Through a set of lilac lines,
and dawn, and dusk,
you look sideways.
Sweet, invasive and entirely silenced thing,
I've company to place beside you –
not yet.
Passerine bird,
in your passage from Persian to English
you're no longer a nightingale, though you'll warble
and curl your toes.
While you perch,
I'm minded to bring you a tree and a night
and a song to be yours: the memorable one
flung out by your namesake from a moonstruck twig
that time our deaths were forecast on the news
so we went for a walk, and rested in you
our everything lyrical forever.

MUSEUM STANDS IN

Room 32, 'India from AD 600', former layout of
Ashmolean Museum, Oxford

...for lone student mandir.
Arrived in the era of paper
with no means of making fire,
I searched— how long?
This was pre-Internet.
Just the telephone book,
its ringbark absence of marble.
So: the museum, in lieu of a temple.
In these my gods' basement days,
stone seemed torn wildly:
Nobody was using this archway,
whispered a disappeared jungle.
Now with renewal, removal,
my gods have changed their storey:
scarlet walls and ochre,
flat-out perilous, higher
than height. The face from a tower
eyeballs my thought towards hugeness.
A ceiling boss of swordsmen
rearrayed, redraws me.
The opening circles of sight...

A TABLE OF MY OWN

Still life by Jan Jansz van de Velde III.
Ashmolean Museum, Oxford

In the year of my marriage, Galileo died.
No man is a solar system.
My days turn full round women averagely called Margaret.
I long to be isolate.
They screw pearls into casements; launder clavichords in pails.
I'm naught, a nutshell castaway.
There are sailing men who've swilled and shot alongside she-pirates.
My father's hands show blue its green.
He harbours precision like a siege device.
No sun in my canvas.
No skull competitively spitting orangepeel.
No silence-broken cittern schooled to lose its strings.
Just night.
This night, which is to me like a cheeseshop to a mouse.
It fills a corner.

After a game with rough fellows,
a single glass.
This glass,
oh it is the measure of my universe.
Till now I had not known
the meaning of adoration.
I drink like an astronomer
at a table of my own.

LATONA AND HER CHILDREN

Latona and her Children. Tapestry in which the heads of men were woven as frogs then altered to human. Ashmolean Museum, Oxford

This tapestry's in sympathy
with wives who have been wronged
in gorgeous-feeling houses
where rage bindweeds into rugs.
You could lay your cheek against this
woolly silky rosy thread,
smug in a censored village
where the frogs have been erased.
   Don't wronged wives, left to themselves,
take revenge, dance, and ride clouds?
   Isn't the mister the victim;
isn't the mistress two-timing,
selfish enough to take up
place after place in the picture;
between being beloved and being
thrown out; however sweet, secret,
the field or grove – it's about her
hoping to stop to drop
bastard fruit.
   The lovely Dutchmen
didn't, perhaps, comprehend
the wolfish desperation
or womanly rude behaviour
of goddesses, in their design.
They put pleasure in the border:
green, without drama; abundant
pears breasting out; a laughing dog,
reassuring woodland décor –
the signs of Artemis to come,
she who reclaims the forest,
untroubled as her father,
fierce as her titan mother.

DOG OR WOLF

Lucera bronzes. Ashmolean Museum, Oxford

Dog or wolf.

Verse, or prose.

I choose to sing to the hairless
who silken my path with their killings,
my hills and plains being pitted
with cattle and cities and middens.
They reek of nerves, arrogant.
I raise my nose, jubilant.
We crouch, we loom.

An agglomeration of moons tumbles through my glottis / Mistress /
I yawn and obey / mooncommands / dawn to musk / night and
sight / fall and water / sheep and herd / the eye-stalk-chase motor
pattern homologue / moonrules Mistress / discipline or perish /
verse and prose.

Who'll choose to croon to the hairless?
Who's wounding? Who's sounding? Who's pooling?
Who reeks of grass, ruminant?
Who'll rise as noise, ululant?

Mistress / I set up a gentle howling / tomb or toy / and now I am
about / wyrd or ward / now I am wholly towards / play or prey / ave,
vale / which is it to be, Huntress?

I hear with ears that point upwards.
Eagerness valleys my backbone.
Satisfaction curls over my tail.
Good lupo; optimum dog.

THROUGH & THROUGH

for Helen Macdonald

I. LATTIMO

Lattimo: milk twist, mist hint.
Venetians pearled minerals –
lead, lime, tin lime – thicked
clear glass to quasi-Chinese
porcelain for simple painting,
birds & flowers. Fingers twirl
composite stems whose colour
twist rock-candies, snake-ladders
precious yellow, less-rare green,
birdclaw red, while blue, longed-for,
yearns like a certainty
expressed by convolution
but inwardly a wynd of truth.
Contemplate, for a moment
(*l'attimo*), how just as when
incalmo joins bubbles blown
separately – two, while hot,
made one – each listed item
here desires liquid, lips;
lights prunted below looped eyes.

II. THE CHOMSKY BEQUEST: TOWARDS A GRAMMAR FROM EIGHTEENTH-CENTURY GLASS

Opaque-twist rival stems home supersubtly.
Clarion teardrop minnows spiral heavily.
Strokable dancing ponds recline pastorally.
Expensive delicate kundalinis amaze unironically.
Triple annular knops preside reticently.
Borderline armed arches lull ruinously.
Diamond-point square afterthoughts quaff piratically.
Milky skippy vignettes land militantly.
Flammable wheeling sisters grave triumphantly.
Colourless green ideals double readily.
Rich fragile blues yellow desirably.
Convex concave shapes flow transparently,
substantially, between pure & empty, between thine & thee.

III. KINGCUPS & CRYSTAL FRIT

The first move: violence to quiet: with having cut stone.
The second move: blank to dayclean: from having cut stone.
The third move: wall to window: having arches cut, of stone.
Establish these and every subsequent move: after violence, such quiet.

Censor   anthemion   memory   azur   or
what   ever   happened   manifestly   show
via   pietra   dolce   snow   grey
leopard   inserts   small   rain   confounding
clear   light   dapples   flayed   down

Let lengths of watered glass into the arches.
Let light be cut so clarity is partial.
This is the way to the mezzanine level.
This is the height of permissible vision.
This is the plan for a balanced landing.

FIAT ◊ SUCCESS ◊ ENTERPRISE ◊ DEFIANCE ◊ EAGLE

… inscription … diamond-point … added after … wheel-engraving,
as if such glass were first engraved with ships
and then
dedicated to order

IV. WINEGLASS

which of the glassmaker family   (lipped ogee bowl)   did this: was
                                                it her,
or   (strong)   him?   (honeycomb moulding)   hard to tell their
                                                wares apart...
she's not   (set)   so good, yet   (knop)
this wineglass is   (plain)   pleasing,   (domed)   a
an aerated helmet   (honeycomb)   dinted all over,   (moulded)   as i-
if grapes wanted defence   (section)   wherever   (triple)   a
a finger might   (annular)   press   (on)   as i-
if fingers wanted a whole   (over)   bunch of dimples   (on)   a
where they could, as if naturally, thoughtlessly purple to rest...
a grappe of glass the reason the wine
remains contained; this breakable stuff,
some barrier to spills, is modelled on bliss
that's thin-skinned, sweetest when burst...
can you compare this? a traditional shape?

CIRCLE

Lamentable, *light sculpture by François Morellet*

A circle lands on the meadow of the retina,
is instantly invisible – because symbolic:
eternity, maternity: not geometric.
Who is mathematical enough to let it be?

The beautiful circle taken apart into arcs
becomes *Lamentable*, pitiable, miserable.
The human who conceived my installation said so,
careful, audible, playful, unfalsifiable.

Tangent: the bright trust in which you go about, reach out,
seems no different from stupidity to those who plan
murders.
     Mercury, argon, phosphor: the triple soul
breathed into me so I glow for you but differently,
differently, unbreathably.
In tinnitus and incandescence
                  mind hazards forms
I spin every which way.
               The sphere tears, taking, fire, free
the sphere held implicit in me holds out for roundness,
fills, collides with light bridged between remembering eyes.
               Oh your heads are waters,
and your eyes a fountain of tears! I weep day and night
for how we are made of breakable and borrowed curves,
my dear ones, my visitors, my several clay reflections.

I sit among you like one of you, approachable
my lap an atlantis ideogram, unfathomable
my other lap a Jacob's ladderbase;
our lit looks climbing into spiderlily embrace.

KISKADEE

80 Roberts Street, Port of Spain

Alice Yard an aviary:
yellow gets up from the gutter,
off the walls, where street light shines,
percolates a milliard miles
out of stars, to come alive
as half thought, half sight,
wholly voice: as birds
whose movement superdivides
human time, irrigated
land, semi-open forest,
terrorises passerines,
sharpens roof-eaves, coconut fronds,
proliferates, preferring
less dense, less dry company.
So imagine Alice Yard
an aviary: every gate,
grid, grille, lock, key, alterable
level, pock-marked wall, concrete
irregularity, soft
and hung over with gauze, full
of uncrushable feathers,
inlaid with night like water,
each person's least move opening
aleatory yellow mirrors,
many presents, one time.

VENUS AS A BEAR:
THE CABIN BOY'S PRAYER

Old Royal Naval College, Greenwich

Because I'm no historian, not even a historian d'amour, marble statues set me dreaming, and I don't care to probe the why or wherefore of Lord Nelson's last words, 'Kiss me, Hardy.' Because, you see, I spent time between the market and the Cutty Sark, where the Guildhall meets the river fog and takes on college shape, and there's a dedicated chapel full of marble caramel, salted with statues of at-risk youth, the trafficked, the fanatics, then known as cabin boys. And I could hear the boys' songs, treble, breaking, broken, 'I'm just a little cabin boy whom Venus has forgot. Oh yes, I love the Lord. The Lord, he is well spoken. He wipes his nose on cambric; I wipe mine on my sleeve. But when the mandatory rum's meridional in my brain and limbs, oh, then I can believe, I'm not a little cabin boy whom Venus has forgot...' For they believed in duty; yes, in Venus as a bear; wanted a manifestation; wanted Venus to give salvation; yes, Venus as a bear.

THE ANTONINE WALL

I. ROME'S NORTH-WESTERN FRONTIER:
INVITATION TO A CIVILISATION

Imp. Caesar's invitation to the ballista ball
by way of white lead acorn-shaped slingbolts arrives
via red-hot correspondence personally stamped,
launches like a no-shit eagle wreathing overhead;
promises ornate south-facing distance slabs, burnt wheat.
Come on. For ages some of you've aped our style, pleading
continuity in Ciceronian Latin
taught at your good school in Wales. You look Celtic and sound
dead. We were hardly dancing when, from the Forth to the Clyde,
thirty-seven miles, evenly, with our differing feet –
Roman contingents of Syrian archers, Roman bands
of Tungrian horsemen – we paced off, or measured, squares.
Now from within the water-to-water wall patrolled
at sky height and from the adverse mouths of platformed fires,
we, between micaceous sandstone pillars, glittering,
ready with an ecumenical flamen,
you, wild, solitary, crafty, literate tribes
invite to a civilisation. You understand.
Stone flows from the hair of snakes where gorgons' heads adorn
both knees of Mars advancing. You're still good on the ground.

II. ROMANO-CELTIC CONTACT IN THE ANTONINE DISPLAY, HUNTERIAN MUSEUM, GLASGOW

I want you like I want a wall
I want you in bits
I take you
underground
your masonry in pieces
I remaster
round house from square fortlet
souterrain from tax gate
Farmers
find pillars
that
retreating
you threw down wells
covered
with small fittings
nails capitals building debris

If litter and landfill were the sum of your legacy
I'd not trouble myself to collect slabs that you cut
sometimes with my hands, so stone fledged warbling; nor myself,
another trophy in this Hunterian hall, flay time
where stone seems just setting from a recent fiery tear,
Roman bones like gaming counters coraled in a jar.

III. FORTUNA, WITH CORNUCOPIA, FOUND AT CASTLECARY BY CANAL WORKERS IN 1769

It is a wall they raised
thrice the height
of rational houses
a wall or a wave is it

turf atop
stone coursework
tidal disastrous
atop tilled fields

Was it Fortuna to guard
stonily liquid
the soapy Romans
It was Fortuna they carved

She was their luck
to light on
to fall from
She was someone you once knew at home

LEAVES/FEUILLES/FALLS

hommage to Pierre de Ronsard, Ode à Cassandre

(i)   Qui   m'a

                      vo

                      lé

      ma

                                fleur

                      verte

                      c'est   la vie

(ii)   This picks up bits of pink
and not quite silverblue
like a glass you drink from
too early, and set down
too low, outdoors, in grass,
so ice water spills on
dew but does not mingle
to make colours; it runs
away, that is clear; so
do you, standing between
sunlight and sight, stamp out
memory; something unfolds
in violets, warmcold throats.

I want the fighter planes
to stay so far away
children crayon them grey
and without accuracy;
right now I pretend

the seedhead of this rose –
infertile, startling gold –
is something I could paint
and not lament; soil
cracks inside, under, you.

Black is what you swim in
when the womb's machinery
rolls rolled-up you about.
We'll swim like that again.
Can we agree on that?

A silk piece, a limepeel,
a sticky-edged table.
A ribbon, a lemon,
a cigarette paper.
A house you get out of
yet cannot get into.
A softness you don't miss
yet one day may long for.
Not having known kindness.
Your taste running to salt.
Reduced to insurance
against dreams or memories,
a wash of green, ashes,
you have no preference.

A very thin whistle,
very old, snapped underfoot.
I picked up the bits.
They once had been painted.

(iii)   voile   pale   velours
               misted   soie   perverse
               lily   lâche   mask
               noble   aster   mure
               cramoisie   iffy
               sage   floral
               cut   cruauté
               souplesse   fall

(iv)   the sunrise hides you
               in layers, slippers,
               and powders of nude

               the man who's singing
               frightened you with how
               your family died

               petal, he called you.
               lass unparalleled,
               selkie, pearl oyster.

               he tells you an earth
               of exclusive loss
               lying and laying.

               shall i uproot you
               with one green look,
               or hand you scissors,
               the twin blades mirrors
               as sharp and partial
               as the view you take from a vase?

(v)   rose in chosen aloneness

        marvellous and unequal

        bounce into self-consciousness

        because you're going too fast

TWO FOREIGN

if this language is the sole
to carry over
how we were war-thrown,
tens, dizzens, thon thorn
honour a tension,
learnt our statues: lesteners,
let's lessen to poems:
but these words have class issues;
is it she'd rase or e-race
unnatural disasters? swap
swamp? fir Deccan,
deckhand? white-wipe? it izny
that; I do clean my ears; wait,
today I past the sign Youth
Redemption Centre, weighed,
Information, end lessoned
to the museum pornograph.
Phono-, okay. A sign tune
status, settle and lessen:
this is a poultry deering,
farm form; rede light and gleenright,
port and porch; born with cattle
or with a caul, see
her, hear mon pote, I don't care,
for forlorner for longer
the stjörnu I stjeer by
wanted from the sky
vaultlines, wed've vound nae fault,
why'd –d I width us?

FOUR PRESENTS WITH PETRARCH

'Son animali al mondo de sì altera
vista che 'ncontra 'l sol pur si difende…'
(*Rime sparse 19*)

I.   Ill and inky, like a beast
     but weaker, and lacking all sense
     except to go towards the light –
     which makes You like a dying sight –
     i burn myself; helpless, You act
     like fire. This fact admits no fault:
     You hurt me, and i seek it out.

II. Sunny animal, delicious almond, salty-eared, earth-shy, sound-
     ing the heights of some uncommon psaltery, don't sigh:
         visitors can't cope – lose the trail – your gold defensive stars
     contrastive and diffuse as seeds, melting into cities, trapped,
     later alter, childrening grain not to be found out; dear,
         trepidatious, grand-limbed trees trialling chilly hatches fan
     into disconsolate bearing, versicular being, and
         no exit further, perhaps, than lassitude signs, shades off –
     not confusion, I don't know what, flowers; evening, poured
     out alone.

     Madder than all others called fool, fingers singed on zarf-free
     coffee, sparring,
         forcing proofs from whichever fellow questions your splen-
     dour, joyful like a circus seal, with a seaside joy,
         suddenly uncollared and crowding to flipper every inlet,
     channel, in-between inish, bocas, up to Ultima Thule itself,
         I journey on a loving quest, absolute, desirous.

I'm inclined to say: doesn't matter what we do, it won't count. Showing you're keen? Being loud? Feeling lucky? You'll be screened out.

Give up. Sit in the dark. Sing scales. Keep imaginary pets.

Delay the thousand bells clicking into cliché. Descend into your most fortified aspect: far-off adoration. Deep in your control I'm lined, love's immigrant citizen. Delighting in you peels and sears me. Safety was fabrication.

Percussion: uncool, non-stop glockenspiel orchestras raindrop unseen from fenced-off and sullen self-gaslighting eyelids: co-co-la-la, lagging legal signatories come firm up the grime of long grief – who can; me, me,

me, with a revolver; I'm that cat, the most modest, most modish catch, with a view to capture – no, you've caught – we're neither of us what it says on the tin; have we conned each other? hey? darling! O, ave my marian rose? I vehemently deny deciding which of us is the duke, which the duchess.

So be it. It's a bargain. So. Don't you want it? Soberly I vow: going both ways or my way, we've got each other going, ravenous, a kite aflame with a petrol tailmate, we're killing it, intravenous, you've made it, I've got you inside my veins.

III.

sun	fun
lurk	dark
run	stun
most	last
ah	ah
least	release
lemming	
gleaming	

IV.   Definite animals
dart into & out of
these poems. 'Thicken up
the description! So: prize
money's what you're after?'
says Paymaster Access.
Thin as lightning tigers,
truly on-the-ground reportage
or your patience,
lady, lord! I commit
excesses, up the dante
content, no win, no fee,
no free street lighting –
roomed in your woods, I burn.

AFTER CATULLUS 5

'Vivamus mea Lesbia, atque amemus…'

Was a time, Catullus, i'd indulge
your counting fetish.
relay how long
        a pause
             i'd need
ascending stairs
        to bed:
squidge. wipe. repeat.
sensation strigilled my declining body.
switched on hyper sensitivities
to linen thread. count.
not to say stone.
till skin inclined to flinch from
sucking-disks. remora-like. which swarm.
from any contact. every surface.
you write when you're cross.
                  sharp. silk.
you're a cultured man.
             dressing
made to measure.
          rubbing
those bronze balls on your abacus.
spittle kissing mercury
on your practice-mirror.
as for me:
        i'm lying
           open,
                 beautifully open,
to a tease of a beautician's
innumerable tweezings.
laughing with the blonde from Gallia

who lays her head
low on my belly
while she tends my lady-garden.

BULLSHIT

How to 'lose' or 'abandon' a word? Put it in jail, throw away the key? Then in every reference book or text block, an opaque rectangle shining where it used to be; a myriad lids to a single oubliette. A fort cut out of yellow, living rock; the particular sightlessness that, with the tide, saturates the underground chamber. This is 'having a concrete imagination'. Not breezeblocks. Wet stuff, instantly; ready to be footprinted.

'Bullshit' is the word I would ease into pasture. One year in an élite institution, my progressive male colleagues kept saying 'Bullshit!' They would get me alone; lean in; ask the really-really-really questions. A little way into my her-answers, they would roar in my face: 'Bullshit!' Eyes pared, jaws gaping, a warlock pack of Jacks of Clubs.

If I seemed quiet, it was because of what I was seeing.

Near my childhood home in a new city, a bull is being led down from the low hills. He walks through the diplomatic area to an empty lot. His haunches a big black valentine, swaying. He dumps as he goes. The asphalt doubly steaming.

A great bull is shitting on my street. Let him have quiet enjoyment.

AFTER *HÁVAMÁL*

> *Deyr fé,*
> *deyja frændr,*
> *deyr sjálfr it sama*

A guest brings lilies.
Not daylilies/hemerocallis;
not alstroemeria, nor lilium regale.
Sweet and wooden. A horse that must be ridden.
The least childlike. Heavier than freesias.
Stargazers. Guests trigger birthday.
Imprinting lilies.

The gift of a book –
Any book is a gift,
bringing time; with no time to read it,
the reader has time, unreading the book,
time implicated in its binding, its petals.
Every book is comprised of one brushstroke.
Needing no witness.

The author is accused.
Accused, repeats the accusation
in print: a narcissist,
the author self-accused of narcissism.
The accusation is a reprint.
The book without footprints. But, yeah.
A smouldering yeahbook.

Things you can count on:
pets dying; people keeling over;
property seizures and repossessions;
the loops and links of the supply chain broken;
places and placenames, small and big, blotted out.
Memento will ride out again as a verb.
Compulsive translation.

EVOLVING @

quick, my snail fist leaks ink:
a towards needs added
at each – atta monkey,
thinks the monk; at one sweep,
pull the tail through, count up
each unit, not round up;
send how many of – it,
clay amphoræ, shipments.

de-systematise the
itemisable in-
describable symbol;
de-handle the handle,
uncoil its dalí yous.
good, goods. key queue croissant.
hover over – whatcha
got? the aerial view
of a sleeping beastie,
cochlea of a boat.

NOVENA BODY PARTS

after Loretta Collins-Klobah, Novena a la Reina María Lionza
(The Twelve-foot Neon Woman, 2011)

NOVENA BODY PARTS: I

Refraction

stars   breath
    T   nip   ples   C
    O   a   bone   A
    R   human   hip   S
    S   I
    O   pum-pum   N
                                 G

ankles   anaconda
          feet

NOVENA BODY PARTS: II

bikini body
deflated, buckled corpse
prostrate plantains ... their green hands
her hammock
into god's lungs!

NOVENA BODY PARTS: III

after the evil eyes of the storms have seen all they want
of our island, …
…
…   each psyche is flood

            children – faces covered with cloths
            eleven bodies – floating in his house
                babies made – babies lost

NOVENA BODY PARTS: IV

NO   the belly   a   boa constrictor   NO

S   his shape   hot feet of a woman   A   H
P   R   U
E   hip bones   T   M
E   I   A
C   C   N
H   ~~speech~~   U
                                                            L
                     trees   A
                                                            T
                                                            E

NOVENA BODY PARTS: V

city, city, city, city, city, city, city,
I, I, I, I, I, I,
of hand, of heart, of desire on my back

jardín botánico
on my inner eyelids
city, its fists,
my business suit

when   light   leaves

NOVENA BODY PARTS: VI

in   the   belly   of   a   snake
trace
taste
dip
do not want to stop...

NOVENA BODY PARTS: VII

girl   snake
   figurine   Reina
    diosa   naturaleza
  running binding   vine ankle
   shed   skin
    ~~sheaf~~   ~~novena~~
  depressions forming off

NOVENA BODY PARTS: VIII

belly   crown   heart
    green hearts
   un hoyo   ancho
  a straight spine

NOVENA BODY PARTS: IX

  our night breaths
        Orion's red shoulder
our bodies revived
      lips
nuzzling   your palm
   a green-heart place
  snake   sanctuary   and...

TIC TAC TOE

Dún Laoghaire pier: two men, as dark as I am, each playing an accordion, next to each other, brotherly, calling hello to the dogs that, preferring squeezebox conversation to the pursuit of seagulls, bark back.

X X X
X X X
X X X

The benches are painted sky-blue, the sky manifestly pearl-grey, the lichens as orange as lifebuoys, the lifebuoys bobbing like blood oranges, the locks do not weep nor bleed rust, the rust looks as natural as metal, if James Joyce's snot was as green as this harbour he must have been snorting powdered kelp and copper, the oxygen makes me asleep, the phone calls out like a clock, and when I arrive inside the Lexicon the studio's shut and the poets beginning.

O O O
O O O
O O O

The question at home is how many lambs this early; which is not my home, nor my question; and like an unlikely birth I poodle along on welcome, uncertain feet.

X O X
O X O
O O X

TENDING

A fast-breathed lamb
is brought indoors.
Illness incandesces
in a cardboard box.
An infrared lamp –
a ruby glass blown womb –
lit, the shock slows
waits, the head lifts.
And if it is enough
or not enough
to strengthen
any one thing,
it is life,
both given and fought for;
it is love,
both granite and meadow.

SALTHILL BLUE FOR MR LAUGHLIN

Thinking unlike a poet,
quit making it new
or dragging netted memories
for the breathless why
this milky blue is also
taffeta, a sheen
of pouring fabric
beyond a purchaser's means.
The sea creeps up on walking,
on the unsinkable sun,
shoes unburying seaweed,
sandworms burrowing down.

INISHBOFIN: I

for Rebecca Barr

A stranger bringing water to a stranger.
One unlocked house among all unlocked houses.
A line of stone along a line of clover.
Beyond a road with stone and clover edges
A looked-for line between wet sky and water
Seams non-existence: large and swift, headed out,
Disappeared in a tilting and a pouring.
How have I been so stupid and not known this?
Heaven most probably is underwater,
Sounding with ease, increasing pressure on us.
Too light for many stars. Too soon for most birds.
Crex crex: a hidden and unvarnished corncrake.
Some way ahead, Rebecca in the pink.

INISHBOFIN: II

for Deirdre Ní Chonghaile

You do just have to listen to the boatman.
Let the boatman make the decision.

INISHBOFIN: III

for Bernard O'Donoghue

The road goes two ways: right and left,
obvious, the bright white dust;
sure as last year and yesterday,
the harbour where friends disembark
without confusion for the climb
towards the hall on the small hill.
Nothing is interchangeable:
shop, slope, feelproof bone called sand,
variant seaweed, boundary stones.
Dark-sailed and unmistakable.
This man walking from inside light
to outside. Fierce, eventful brain.
Leader through telescopic fields.
Yet if kindness walked with flags,
he'd still be taller.
    Like a child
old age is not, and he is not –
He has stopped. And here it starts:
'I very easily get lost.'
A voice of great sweetness and trust.
Nothing is interchangeable.
This exercise that hurts the heart.
Red-hulled and unmistakable.

INISHBOFIN: IV

sea for a bit
lovingly lifting it off
this felted skin
this roof needing resurfaced

SEASTAIRWAY

'ofer wapema gebind'
The Wanderer

We sail

a~a~a~the~the~the~the
sea-troughs~sea-tombs~seawalls
the~the~the~the~this~that~my
seafarer~seawalker~seasaint
her~their~sea-lamb~seafriend
wandered~outlined~holy~crowded

    wait for it: waiting occurs
    in waves *put up and shut up*
    the hand is undomestic
    at this scale: ice-dipped, might be
    a beak, cormorant, gannet;
    might be a scientific   with~seabelled~seanight
    instrument, ice-proof; is in   in~seaful~seawind
    a bind. you know, if you know,   searoped~sea-
tongued~seagreat
    you'll *put up and shut up*. sleep   over~seabord~seaside
    only, sleep alone, brings hands
  down~seamist~seagrain
    out of the scale of exile;   seacircling~seabraes~sea-
gentled
seaskin~early-white-haired
furious~sea-martyrdom~worth
seawork~surrounding~searopes
beside~emerald~seadeep~sea-show
sea-marching~to~sealaw~into
seaside's~seabent~seawalls

fingerprints, in dreams, become
warmth in warmth, identified
and not identifiers.
　who laps the swing of a sky
seastrolling~find~seadoors
　　where triumph and vertigo　　　into~seashelled~pulses
　　don't lock down on darker eyes?
　sealogged~seachanged~through
　　　　　　　　　　calling~seaware~seavessels
　　　　　　　　　　lie~break~seanight's
　　　　　　　　　　endured~seavessel~moves

seadogged~scaled~reined
bubbled~filled~wrecked
skidding~seafared~on
whispered~　　　*put up and shut up*. the gold
well~　　　　　of a horse of dreams canters
only~　　　　　the inheld field of my blood.
　　　　　　　in your museums, I found
　　　　　　　me, lady, right at your side.

seaport

WATERLOO, TRINIDAD

a lignum vitæ lion's head carving misused
as a water spout corrupts aligns with bamboos
cotton flags linked marigolds these temple discards
poking out from where the waterline meets
concrete painted idols' eyes lolling too three six
twenty times over and the tide does not wash them
rather fades the boundaries of impurity and
pietry, truth and tourism, while picnicking
pyramid-ribbed dogs run among cars given as bribes
to humans lesser than ministers, greater
than market vendors, all whose prayers cast red powders,
none owning (who owns) the fast boats gunning orders.

STRONG AS ROSES

Since he died, who keeps moving the box
with the priest things: white fire-candy,
camphor; the left-handed conch to blow?
Since they died, who will water the plants
in pots painted serpent-blue: beauty-
and-the-beast roses?

Since this house lies low
in the sinking north, who put something
so scented as to impose
an outdoors larger than the indoors,
garden in a single room,
smells of hallucinatory roses?

When traced, this blossoming reaches back
to a forgetting in cotton clothes.
A packet of Sri Lankan incense.
What hot conditions, concentrated
method grow into such thickness
that, sealed, unseals flame powered by roses?

TRINIDAD SUGAR

Like winged seeds, ashes glide and settle;
the air multiform, populated,
a bright puzzle, ten thousand pieces,
a busy mezzanine above the gardens,
the capital, the hills, the highway;
the ashy air seeded with leaf trash.

The child has gone into the house.
The fields have been set on fire.
The snakes escape like wilder roots.
Only the serried cane stands, proofed by its juice;
having arrowed, not flowered.
Few clearing processes are fiercer.

A Murano swan sails from Venezuela.
A spun sugar eagle sails from Florida.
An emerald fortress sails from Demerara.
Fields having been levelled for housing,
snakes seeking rebirth in old drainpipes,
and a different white powder taking fire.

The child has grown taller than the table.
Sieved through incinerated bones of cattle,
sugar sails for export from America.
Slavery days are over.
In the heritage-industry kitchen,
a web-linked grandmother makes fudge.

MOSS, FOR MAYA

I. A child left alone can befriend moss. Its bright green, enticing to the eye as a lemon lolly behind the teeth, makes moss seem to shine in the darkness under lizard-haunted ixora bushes & on the killing patch of concrete that disaffected workmen splashed on earth that had been alive with wet-combed roots, as if extermination were necessary for human habitation, & moss an infiltrator.

II. Moss has not tiny tongues, nor little fingers, nor flames fine as watchmakers' tools, nor an elfin semaphore system. Moss is not-lickable, not-glossolalia, not in-the-way-on-the-way. Moss is myriad, simply many & one. Moss absorbs.

III. For the benefit of giants, fourteen kinds of Icelandic moss were exhibited under glass, including the static flicker of a moss named for its resemblance to white worms, a name mistranslatable as 'pale dragons'. It must have been plucked from the cooled flowing lava fields that look like nothing, yet where detail thrives – clumps of pink carnivorous daisies, trapping zippy insect life.

IV. The life cycle of moss is momentous. Any given colony of moss could have been there since whichever chosen beginning, while changing at a rate that puts mammals' eyes to shame.

V. Don't slip. Grab the balustrade. Don't slip. She's broken her arm. Don't scrape too much off. It's beautiful. Bleach it all off. It's a risk. Coexist. Moss exists. Our stone selves roll on different tracks, unmatchably cracked. We cling. Resist. Shape to our ends whatever is. Not this. Moss induces words in us because, grave & new, we sentence things; whereas moss carpets, respires, pulls back, is.

ORCHIDS, FOR MAYA

I. Said the text: man (*sic*) made in image & likeness of God; by
    implication, animals apart. Not a part. Distanced. Unlike.
    Not dislike. Useful. Supplicant, ever, not to cross into
    dead; into food. Supplicant. Supply. Succulent. Yet man
    (*sic*) ranges & ravishes his (*sic*) likeness out of every bit of
    the palpitant, breath-holding world: will palpate a breast
    of stone to tear out heartsblood, 'hæmatite'; will pursue a
    roaming softness till it yields a shielded being, 'hermit crab';
    overtopped by wondrous flowers, will dig for tubers & find
    testicles. *Orkhis*. It's his (*sic*) fantasy. Voilà, the bridal orchid,
    coyly masculinised at its roots.

II. & I was not, was not a namer, was not Abrahamic, was a
    traveller, was metempsychotic before meeting that word, was
    unworlded & reworlded indianly soul by soul, which I (it)
    did not believe, yet I (it) passed this present consciousness
    into those things that mattered because I (it) was placed be-
    fore them to wait, as a child waits & changes while, because,
    waiting; before I (it) caught the trick of rising out of any sit-
    uation like soluble particles, I (it) would go for all or nothing,
    for the narrative voice, for characterless, bounding atmos-
    phere. So: this orchid. It (not-I) is outside. I (not-it) crush
    up against the words for it, the seeing a saying, the display
    a don't touch, as a wanting face & sexy hands flatten against
    shatterproof glass, making this human spring a reflection,
    this vegetal yearning for connexion always pluckable, already
    englobed, a singular narcissus heeled by a soapy panic, a stark
    desire clouded by echoing aldehydes. I (it) am built to be the
    outside. O to take it in. It, it is.

III. Three orchids: yellow tintinnabulation high up in a tent in
     Trinidad, a sweeter chime before the prizewinning frighten-
     ing yams, first time this word orchid thing.

IV. Three orchids: the second, knowable as a quiet & agile slight disruption, snake-like, to the line of a tree's bough, spiderlike in being mottled purplegreen, another colour too not chestnut nor livid just vitally deep nameless colour of orchid-flesh, orchid who by sprouting silently to us though perhaps not silently to all sorts of differently sensing things living at different pitches and paces, orchid who therefore makes this garden a space though walled up to a point after that point open-air, something goes, anything grows, wild.

V. Three orchids: disconnect served snapped aphrodisiac on the edge of a dish a challenge for mauve-balled males o what have you come to, third forest flower, jammed with tines, thigh cuisine, arts supplement opener under artificial night?

SEED, FOR MAYA

I.   the voice of the seed

II.   you said

III.   as yet it has no voice

IV.   the seed
perhaps ever

V.   a star, a trap, a tropism, a keep,
a wrinkle, a tide; these voiced weirds; (k)not
so sweet stone, so liquid seed

HEIRLOOM ROSE, FOR MAYA

heirloom rose argument: in which way a flower could be an
heirloom? via dna only or the price of hybridised flowers, i.e.
replicability not uniqueness, & punishment of (culling/killing
of) such specimens as fail to conform – in a garden with wet grass
swishing round one's ankles, looking up at roses, to look up a
pain in the neck & a posture of worship, at expensive roses, frail,
with pests beaten off by invisibilised gardeners, on always some-
one else's secretly bloodied historical brick or stone wall (such
masonry) – returning to the replicability of the heirloom rose,
especially as roses are more or less infertile, their seed minuscule,
dry, produced like dust by a perfect, empty room/womb dead/
head, yes, returning to the replicability, it could be because any
rose (gulab) is as sweet as any other rose, in so far as the rose it-
self queens it over us by sheer assertion of rose-ness, the way the
cheapest plastic tiny Taj Mahal model in the post office corner
shop still transfixes purchasers because it means India, the post
office factual location shelved and overcome by the idea of an
historical palace, which we also know to be distant, which means
what is overcome too is the idea of the object's nearness: to buy
it is to buy into faraway, it is a magic object, & for similar rea-
sons every rose works magic – however, handiwork, chairbacks,
heirloom, loom, woven, tapestried, needlepoint, wool, women's
fingers, flattened, passed down, designed for living, restored as
when made by the dead, heirloom rose n'a rien à voir with the
jardin mais plutôt is a rose de l'intérieur, creation of shades,
ombrageuse, a rose best left unsunned, fading, faded, a settled-
upon-the-price fabricated rose – the word heirloom makes rose
not verb not rise not and-lilies not catholic not angel virgin mag-
nificat bouquet, rather heraldry, stamps, elfishness, the reddest
rose nonetheless a blonde princess, dangerous, dangerous to me,
rose of heritable identity, not flaming shedding transgressing
parterres and pathways not rose phénix rose curieuse but em-
blem of empire, imperial as natural, pressing away the senses'

write/right to come to the rose as is – you could even make wars under its banner, york or lancaster, roses, rose is, rose isn't, sorry Gertrude Stein, rose exceeds/is in excess of no I mean is exceeded by connotations, with heirloom, of 'rose'.

FOSSIL TRADE, FOR MAYA

fossil	trade	hand	trade
flipper	trade	coil	trade
comet	trade	beam	trade
mother	trade	mote	trade
water	trade	fire	trade
father	trade	dust	trade
drone	trade	wind	trade
bird	trade	bread	trade
bead	trade	breast	trade
trick	trick	or	trade
fossil	clocks	fossil	clasps
trade	plus	trade	pasts

BJÖRK / BIRCH TREE

Take out the silver and the pallor, come out
from under ether, from being reasonable,
come down from being condemned to live behind clouds.
Lady into swan, come down; swan into sea,
set down; fire from the sea, set out; reach; launch.

In the winter in the square near Kjarvalsstaðir,
the only colour burns on birch tree torsos
intense as tribal scars, roughed up like embers,
natural-unnatural mineralic orange;
a silent whiteness whitely dark in daytime,
in self-lit snowlight witness to increasing night,
the birch trees in the square near Kjarvalsstaðir.

Lady into swan, the Icelandic moon is rising
on fourteen kinds of moss, on military
exercises, on the spire people leap from
whose stories may outlast the night. A tribute
is a summons; but who summons trees? They mean suspense,
an ending between chase and chase. Trees grow in pursuit.
A tribute is a summons; but who dismisses trees?
With the moon, a roaring rises, swatting at the air.

CROSSING BORDERS: ASSUMING THE HABITS OF THE DAY AND NIGHT

I.

They saw an infant
jellybaby melds triumphant
into shoulder:
child of elephant
child of mountain
nobody can hold
(*there is no her*) this lighthouse, this arrivant

> Remember the oneness that carried through
> the oneness that carried you
> into being/one with them/not one of them,
> tiny head a candlewick at the cocktail party?
> Looking back, a night of absent childcare
> that first reception; you were not yet two.

★ ★ ★

They saw a child
but you were making the rulebook
from the border:
where road meets slope
where slope meets sea
no driver can go;
(*there are others*) strangers shed clothes, nakedos

> The sea smells of gasoline and chicken
> and vaseline and sun cream,
> iron landslides/cool in nostrils/you bring the sea
> what it smells of; look straight down over unjaded cliffs,
> feel no fear inside of the sheer outside,
> it is also you, you tide in the view.

***

They saw a problem
but it was inside your body
which they could open:
she is too young
she can't have bled
it's an infection;
(*put up your legs*) your brother runs in the door

> Since becoming an examined being,
> you limit your family
> to those whose governance over blobby body
> sends you over its edge; hopping celotex, that's you
> playing across the lines of ceiling tiles,
> easy flying out, less easy staying you

II.

Home is where you close the gate against vagrants / home is where you open the gate to some people you let into the yard / home is where you open the front door to make a fuss of old friends / home is where you open the side door to somebody who tells you about someone else's home and how she did not feel at home because their house was Hindu and your house is not like that / home is where your schoolfriend just became somebody and your house is perfectly inhabited by a second, occasional, garish, obscured house that is Hindu and somewhat like that unknown, complained-about, other person's place / home is where you tricked somebody into being invisibly somewhere that is somewhere she would talk about if only she knew how much where she was is somewhere else / home is where you take off your shoes and leave the dust of the road outside the threshold like the soiled garment of the body is dispersed as ash after cremation / she has taken off her shoes / should you tell her / should

you tell her she has just taken off her shoes / should you tell her
she has not just taken off her shoes / thirteen lunar months run
above twelve solar ones and interweave with them / this is mid-
day / does she know she is safe at midday / does she know the
next day begins at dawn but in this house the next day has also
already begun the previous twilight / will it be safe if she stays
until twilight / when the light switch flicks on to the sound of
sanskrit and your father's voice makes the goddess enter / you
have tricked her by inviting her like in a fairytale but you are not
sure if you are magic or mortal or foreign or which / where is
the border around the so rich field of liking that so far you had
shared

III.

Dar a luz: to be born is to be brought to the light
but do not wish her *feliz cumpleaños*;
do not tell her, either, that I let you know
that in the Spanish Civil War they shot her father
like most of the villagers; did they trespass
or were they pushed into the realm of the no longer mortal
hence unforgettable? The shot was fired
on her birthday; you must remember that
she remembers her date of bringing to light
in the blaze of death.
Anyway you are not supposed to know when a nun's
birthday falls, because they are married
to Christ, and lose their names, and choose a name.
Yes, I think they get to choose. Why does she always wear
nun-shoes? It is part of her habit.
It would be out of order for her to dress otherwise,
being in an Order that wears blue and white,
and travels overseas; she has desired to go
on an awfully big adventure...

IV.

The thing is when one of the men said that martial arts class was nothing but thwarted sexuality and another of the men disagreed because fighting is erotic and theoretically homosocial you could not say a thing.

You could not explain how you have not been in your own skin when you were skin on skin with another human being and indeed had your heads in each other's crotches when stretching after the warm up and before sparring you could not tell him that you do not pause to savour skin on skin or even feel the heat of the other person because having been transformed into a thing that acts as soon as thinks leaves no way back into the experience that lets you back out again to explain.

When the white costume is in motion with such a clean line that it cracks so you hear it you know from the sound like a sound effect there is action that is going right but you cannot see the film and this is not acting when you advance the edge of your arm so the sharp bone blocks it may cause both hurt but causes none pain when you become two metres of direction and two knuckles of surface you are concentrated you may be in contact you are not in touch it is going through you are the maths and machine through which it goes through through when the white costumes are in motion.

V.

Damn you, I said in my head, but also affectionately,
I am not speaking of or as myself or for any/one
when I try to think feelingly into the girls who wear veils.
When you said to me 'outward show', not at all affectionately,
you were not speaking of my wearing white as a token for mourning,
you were thinking that clothing is put on and put off,
is separate from body and body is separate from spirit,
but my every day is a being in of being
a mixity of worlds;

you were deciding that I had choice and had made a fashion choice,
that colour had not run out of my life
such that anciently and in other ugly adverbs and untranslatable
   ways
my body was temporarily and cross-temporally beyond being
   dressed or mine
but was one of all those who were ever like me in mourning;
and if you could have cut me through like a crystal, the truth of
   my insides
would have been colourless too, though you might have decided
to fail to see that clarity
and instead reinvent my lungs and my guts to decipher as crassness,
at which point my ichor and shit would have been your illusion.
There is, too, the amulet
prayed over in front of a thousand-name-chanted fire
by another dead one;
it was like poking my eye or bruising my clit
when the airport guard stared me down
and fingered it as if to pretend
it might be a poison capsule or travestied/radical souvenir bullet,
I felt it hold up my nerves when she grabbed the gold cylinder,
the metal hung in air
clasped externally
yet more internal to me.
So take it off is not an option. Without trying, thinking feelingly,
I am not speaking of or as myself or for any/one.
Damn the subtle body's extension into material, affectively.

CHARLOTTE STREET

this is not to say
she's like a fish
she isn't   you'll think
i've said that she
is   like a fish
   the finding of her
filleted corpse
curled frozen in the
upstairs storage of
the popular shop
might put you off sole,
plaice, and surgical
procedures, yes,
even those paid for
legitimately
   i think no women
are like fish   you will
remember that street
please   for its market
stalls, innocence of
knives, heaping
pumpkins, melons, or
some heavy triumph
i picked for my bag
walking home partway
past the hospital,
the convent school, the
sprung floors of corrupt
government spaces
before calling   you
to come with your car
   just to be sure   i'm
ok   i think   and
i won't   forgive   you
for understanding this

& WHEN DESIRE FOR AIR NOT
PIPED THROUGH FILTERS PICKS UP IN
YOUR URGENT LEGS, REMEMBER

i.m. Juliet Tam, disappeared 1985, Arima, Trinidad

juliet juliet
you're at the end of every street
juliet juliet
i never knew you; where'd you go,
who took you, juliet?
juliet? in your name
they tie my foot; can't leave the house
girl, stay in the yard, girl,
it was less than fifty yards
away she vanished
just just so; juliet ju–

SHE SELLS...BY THE SEA SHORE

let's focus on her fingernails:
silk acrylic they are not.
hardened in mirandrous sunlight,
deft, they clean the littlest ones
first. pinky chip-chips hunted out
from tell-tale blowholes – oh pretty
tunnellers, taking elusive
action, the breathing beach yields up
your sinking spirals directly
as a form of signalling, where
you intended hiding! and so
let's focus on her fingernails,
that won't be accounted dainty
or susceptible to wounding
by sun, salt, cuts; at least, not when
compared to pearled hands that shell out,
peeled, preferentially currencied.
nowtime is downtime, attention,
let's focus on her fingernails...

INNOCENTS

it   neat
filtered   as
in   guilt

folds unflying   meek & mild
mouthful sundust   nice to crush

no less   no
than one   less than one
fingernail   pinkie nail

no more   no
than one   more than one
lights as if   nothing soft

one on   one
on or   in
from the   slow mo
floor   on the door

inoffensiveness might look
like this
they crawl   mobled small

lightly landing   land as if
slightly reduced   one moth sifr
sifr moths peel off each fixture

from   bulb
overhead   fittings
set off
as if   settling
so what amounts chhah ocho

the ceiling   drab
yields   bodies

they will not open their wings

between   quinze
tiles   modest
too

why won't they open their wings

are they feeding off the hair
of goats?

finally they pour from   walls
every crevice   being filled full
                      of rock wool
insulation
now irremovably stuff
of moth mothlife & mothdeath
the fabric of the building –

who only wanted to live

where   it is warm

RIDDLES

I.   Chairs. Ruthless cornfield.
Counters. Writless canefield.
Lotus. Lotusless CCTV.
Children. Fingers. Children.
Voices. Children. Dodges.
Self-rearranging furniture.
Polytheist plastic. Christmas.
Treble-clef rug.

II.   Landscape: aeroplanes::
helplessness: fertiliser.
Fear. Change.
What is as beautiful:
local birdwatchers,
in a zone reported
globally for tinpots,
wind, wars.

III.   Fastidious taste.
Calligraphy or graffiti
only. Novels
dead and at length
only. So,
so quick, unprompted
birdsong laughter.
So, so quiet
a step ahead.
Espresso on gelato.
Only contempt
the cold with the turkey.
Only contempt
the trap with the honey.

III.   A horse. A honey.
           Unhurried in sunlight.
           A hiding-place. A hammer.
           I actioned and you felt.
           Hillside and hurtler.
           You let me close.
           On distance. At length.
           Movements of minutes.
           Minutes of hands.
           Minutes of midnight.
           Midnight of hands.
           Hands of crustaceans.
           A seabed a bedside.
           I fled and they sold you.
           A fever a lover.
           Distanced. Not closed.

IV.   Same-sex lover.
           Without the range I need.
           Not lacking cruelty.
           I bleed where you thin out.
           Time-traveller, foreigner,
           whose features bring the Tudors
           closer, belly of dust.
           When you break
           I knot you up.
           We bargained for this.
           Lay you on carpet,
           in your blue bed,
           laid in your coffin.
           Give up on you.
           Hand you over
           to a dead friend's boy.

V.   In this case,
black plastic
back seat.
Red T-shirt
cowling and burning.
In a similar case,
a manicure kit,
biracial monochrome,
double surname,
monastic carpark.
Can you hear –
my friends were those dancers.
– what didn't happen.
With and without.
Portable amps.

THE MAGNIFICENT PIGS OF THETFORD

after Trout Mask Replica, *Captain Beefheart*

One neighbour takes a kayak
on the water meadow.
Two neighbours boot up for a walk,
stare in my window.

This poem didn't happen
in Thetford.

The trick is: look into the lens
as if you're going to shoot it.
Turn your back or make a cheesecake?
Cute doesn't cut it.

This poem happened a long time after
we travelled past Thetford.

Black: I wish I hadn't seen
helicopters like umbrellas.

Thetford is in Norfolk,
a very fine county.

Yellow: I wish I didn't know
the pianist frigs his dog.

I have never lived there.
I have lived in other Fens.

Red: I wish that you would hear
the singing blood in cities.

I have adored East Anglian
birds, flints,
churches, sandwiches,
poets, and pigs.

I built up to say 'Hello',
but it took centuries.

This poem is a Captain Beefheart tribute,
but I can't say it has nothing to do with Thetford.

And now your heart's a frozen chandelier.
I break off a hard teardrop
as reparations.

There were pigs in a farm
like it was a holiday camp.
They had their arms crossed as they leant on the fence
to look out at the world
in Thetford.

A giftwrapped concrete handkerchief
is my garden square.
I unwrap a concrete handkerchief
as my square garden.

The rosy, tanned pigs
looked out and relaxed.

The horizontal neighbours growl
their hunger for my flowers.
I say, this is my square garden.
They say, it's ours,
and underwater.
Marigolds come up like koi carp,

edible and smart.
My roses snip like snappers.
Cosmos astrosanguineus
joins in the transmogrification.
Pæonia suffruticosa
looms, a humongous grouper.

The pigs stood tall in the sun
like they weren't going to be killed.

Nobody comforts a weeping pear.
Nobody scrapes prostrate juniper
up from the floor.

And have forks stuck in their backs,
perhaps in Thetford.

Keep digging willow pattern orts
and Royal Doulton fragments,
bone china and tobacco packets
in my square garden.

A sad contrast with Captain Beefheart's China Pig.

I heard a whisper
deep in the litter of my garden square.
The sweet and reconstituted voice
of a paradisaical coinbox.

Lovingly preserved
His China Pig.

'I've fallen to bits,
but I witness you.
With an oink-oink-kiss,
I'm still here.'

It fed the neighbourhood
and lives forever.

Oh!
What a treasure.

CATGUT

You like them silken.
I'm listening for the looseness:
there's one string in them
cannot be tensed
to the tone they listen for
to the tune you'd disappear
to the note this song needs.

WHEN SITTING IN THE KITCHEN IS LIKE BEING WITHIN THE BODY OF A STRINGED INSTRUMENT WHERE IT JOINS THE NECK

Singing
            it is-   n't   singing
                        singing
in   particular
            it is-   n't
singing   mobile   chaffinch
timer   emergencies   resonant
sing-   ing   hlusten
            it is   singing
                        the house

THE SEETHING SEA

ceaseth the sea   fluid with dead fish
seething the sea   the mind's eye disguises
seemeth the sea   our self instrumental
diamond the sea   warmth, tremor & seeing
the mind's eye   imaged inside machines
the mind's eye   edging a flatfish flubbed
disguises   a lip-curled sea
disguises   an altered skate
read read tonight to night of regions
known holy & only by aeroplane
for vortex read vertex, for phosphorescence
read foreigners, for read read repeat
ah ah thing that does not exist
ah ah children who have run out
for stones read bombs rough stones dear bombs
the sea releasing where from you ways
a poem does not cease a poem does not
ease rough peaks dear poet for speak read seethe

ENVOI

[…] *each your doing,*
So singular in each particular,
Crowns what you are doing in the present deed,
That all your acts are queens.

Shakespeare, *The Winter's Tale* IV. iv.

> green green
> blue green
> tray of arrows
> tray of stars
> my enteared heart
> my enearthed heart
> what would you
> do you know

ACKNOWLEDGEMENTS

Some of these poems were published first in the selection *Seas and Trees* (Canberra: Recent Work Press). Thanks to all involved in the Poetry on the Move Festival, University of Canberra (2017).

Thanks to St John's College, University of Cambridge, whose generosity during my Harper-Wood Studentship (2016–17) made travel possible. Thanks beyond words to the friends before, after, and during the years in Cambridge.

Thanks to the islands festivals – Bocas Litfest, Trinidad and Tobago (Marina Salandy-Brown and Nicholas Laughlin); Inish: Island Conversations, Inishbofin, Republic of Ireland (Peadar King and crew).

Thanks to Douglas Caster, and to the School of English, University of Leeds, where the final stage of work on this book has been supported by the Douglas Caster Cultural Fellowship in Poetry.

Thanks to Calum Gardner.

Gratitude, and apologies for any omissions, to: *Ash*; *Granta*; *PN Review*; *Poetry Wales*; *Stand*; *past simple*; *Poetry at Sangam*; *Wolf*. *Asterism: An Anthology of Poems Inspired by Punctuation* (Laudanum, 2016); *Bad Kid Catullus* (Sidekick, 2017); *Birdbook: Farmland, Heathland, Mountain, Moorland* (Sidekick, 2015); *Birdbook: Saltwater and Shore* (Sidekick, 2016); *Face Down in the Book of Revelations: for Peter Hughes on his 60th Birthday* (Oystercatcher, 2016); *Translating between Sensory and Linguistic Borders: Journeys between Media* (Palgrave Macmillan, 2018); *The Caught Habits of Language* (Donut Press, 2018); *The Polar Tombola: A Book of Banished Words* (Tompkin Press, 2017); *The Red Hen Anthology of Indian Poetry* (Red Hen Press, 2018); *Venus as a bear* (London: Stinky Bear Press, 2013). Alice Yard (with thanks to Kriston Chen, Andre Bagoo, and the Douen Islands collective); 'Auld

Enemies' (with thanks to S.J. Fowler, and Jeremy Noel-Tod); 'Doped in Stunned Mirages: A Poetic Celebration of Don Van Vliet', Bluecoat Gallery (with thanks to Kyle Percy, Chris Mc-Cabe, and Bryan Biggs); Expanded Translation (with thanks to Dr Zoë Skoulding, the University of Bangor, and the AHRC); International Literary Showcase / Norwich Writers' Centre; Performance Philosophy; 'Poetry and Pictures at the Museum' (with thanks to Nick Owen, and to the Ashmolean Museum, Oxford); 'Poetry on the Move', University of Canberra; 'Poets After Dark / Light Show' at the Hayward Gallery, London (with thanks to Bea Colley).

Some of these poems were written in conversation with Loretta Collins Klobah's *The Twelve-foot Neon Woman* (Peepal Tree, 2011), and with Maya Chowdhry's *Fossil* (Peepal Tree, 2016).

All lambs in this book belong to Selina Guinness and Colin Graham of Tibradden and @19acres.